Gasoline On Fire

*Stop Spending Time And Money On
Instagram Marketing Business Strategies That
Don't Work And Start Focusing On
Delivering Leads To Improve Your Revenue*

Justin A. Parker

Bluesource And Friends

This book is brought to you by Bluesource And Friends, a happy book publishing company.

Our motto is **"Happiness Within Pages"**
We promise to deliver amazing value to readers with our books.
We also appreciate honest book reviews from our readers.

Connect with us on our Facebook page www.facebook.com/bluesourceandfriends and stay tuned to our latest book promotions and free giveaways.

Don't forget to claim your **FREE** books!

Brain Teasers:

https://tinyurl.com/karenbrainteasers

Harry Potter Trivia:

https://tinyurl.com/wizardworldtrivia

Sherlock Puzzle Book (Volume 2)

https://tinyurl.com/Sherlockpuzzlebook2

Also check out our best seller books

"67 Lateral Thinking Puzzles"

https://tinyurl.com/thinkingandriddles

"Rookstorm Online Saga"

https://tinyurl.com/rookstorm

Contents

Introduction

Welcome to the world of Instagram – a part of the exciting new means of communication known as "social media".

But as we'll soon find out, Instagram isn't just any old social media platform. It provides an easy way to reach millions of potential customers. In this book, we're going to show you ways that you can use Instagram to build your brand, reach out to new customers, and grow your email lists.

First, we'll begin with a discussion that will cover the whys of Instagram. When you're getting started, you'll want to know why you should divert your precious time devoted to marketing your business over to Instagram.

After we've covered that information, we'll go over the process of creating an Instagram account – something that is deceptively simple but mission-critical. If you mess things up right at the beginning, it's going to be costly to change it later on.

Then, we'll explore some "unwritten rules" of Instagram, so that you understand how to post and interact on the forum. You're going to learn vital strategies that will help you grow your followers and increase brand awareness – and how this will start to translate into sales and cold, hard cash.

Next, we're going to discuss integrating your website and sales funnel into Instagram. You're going to find out that Instagram can become a potent (and low-cost or even free) source of leads. To take advantage of it – you'll need to have your sales funnel and webpage set up just right. We'll discuss the issues that you'll face when doing this.

Gasoline On Fire

Growing your following over time is one of the most important tasks of your business on Instagram. We'll talk about legitimate ways to do this and also explore how to make use of shoutouts from so-called "influencers", and other promotion methods.

Finally, we'll translate SEO into the Instagram world, where the proper use of hashtags can help get your Instagram page found by eager users.

Chapter 1: Why Instagram?

Before we get going on the hows of Instagram, it's important to learn the whys. In this chapter, we're going to describe the platform and explore the main reasons that you'll want to use it to promote your business. If one aspect of your business is collecting leads through online squeeze pages, or if you're marketing affiliate products, your own digital products, online courses, or webinar classes, Instagram is something that can really drive your business to new heights. But why is that? Let's count the ways!

Instagram Has a Huge, Devoted Audience

When I began researching on Instagram, the first statistic that caught my eye was the huge number of monthly active users. The most recent estimates that

Gasoline On Fire

I've seen are that Instagram currently has 650 million active users. That's impressive, but I know that some people are saying, "so what?" Yeah, how many users does Facebook have?

The number of users isn't the only metric of importance. We're also interested in how engaged the users are, how they are likely to react to a marketing pitch, and how much competition there is. Consider this fact – while some 96% of businesses have some presence on Facebook, only about 36% have a presence on Instagram.

Does that mean that you have free reign on Instagram? Well, of course not. But the fact that so many businesses haven't yet gotten on the platform means that it's quite a bit less crowded. When things are less crowded, and not so many businesses are competing for eyeballs, that makes it far easier for small players to have a big impact, and do it more rapidly.

When it comes to younger buyers, Instagram is definitely a place where you want to be marketing. American users who are under the age of 25 are on Instagram on average about a half-an-hour per day. Considering that Instagram is accessed 99.99% on mobile, that is actually a huge number. When people are on smartphones, they have an attention span of a gnat. So, if they are spending half-an-hour with one app on their phones, that is literally a huge amount of time.

If I told you people only watched TV for 30 minutes a day, you would be shocked and probably note that advertising on TV would be a total waste of time. But that would not be the right way to look at Instagram. On Instagram, things are happening in split-second intervals. Think about it: Even with the advent of

Gasoline On Fire

Stories (more on that later, but they are only 15 seconds long anyway), you're talking about things that last a few seconds – like looking at photos.

When it comes to Instagram, remember three things: Simple, fast, and engaging.

Sounds kind of like a paradox, but think about how a stunning photo makes you feel. It's definitely engaging, even if you only look at it for a few seconds, and then swipe on for the next one.

That's part of the opportunity and the challenge with Instagram – you need to have engaging content that immediately catches people. If you do, then the speedy nature of Instagram is going to work in your favor – by helping you rapidly grow and bring in new clients.

We'll be talking about Instagram Stories in a bit, but here is an amazing stat: Every single day, a half a billion people use Instagram Stories. You may not have noticed it – but other marketers have, and they are rapidly finding ways to get in on the Story action.

If that wasn't stunning enough, consider that there are more than 4 billion likes of Instagram posts every single day.

So, this is a very active social media platform, with a large numbers of users, even if their absolute numbers are lower than Facebook.

Instagram is Super Easy to Use

When you learn about Instagram as a business owner, you're going to learn that it's about art as much is it is about science. The platform is deceptively simple. It started out as a photo-sharing service, and although it's evolved somewhat, it remains basically that.

This has its advantages and disadvantages.

The advantage is that the simplicity can make things easier for you as a marketer. If you are able to make some good posts, then you're going to have some success. It's as easy as making a quick photo, or a 15-second video, and uploading it to the app.

The disadvantage is that simplicity leads many business owners and marketers to cut corners. They don't take enough time to pre-plan, and instead go about things in a sloppy fashion. And guess what – their efforts fail.

So, take advantage of simplicity, but don't let it lull you to sleep.

Your Niche is On Instagram

There are more than 650 million people in the world, and obviously, not everyone is on Instagram. But as a business owner, you don't care. What's relevant is that every niche is on Instagram. So, no matter what your niche is, you're more than likely going to be able to exploit Instagram to promote your business. Some of the niches that are on the app include:

- Finance
- Health
- Fitness
- Weight loss and nutrition
- Biz opp
- Self-Development/Motivation
- Pets/Dogs/Horses/Cats
- Entrepreneurship
- Real Estate

- Beauty

And many more. I've only just scratched the surface. The bottom line is, you can use Instagram to find people who are interested in the niche that is your market.

Keep in Mind That it's Mobile

If you're not from Gen Z, one of the hardest things to wrap your mind around might be that Instagram is virtually entirely mobile. It is an app, and you need to think of it that way. Yes, you can log onto the website from a desktop computer, but that is not how people use it. It's estimated that 99.9% of their usage is on mobile devices.

This is a new way of doing things – everything else is cross-platform. Facebook, Twitter, blogs, Amazon – everything else is cross-platform. Not Instagram, though – your users *will* be seeing your stuff on a mobile device. That's important because you are going to need to make sure your business has been adapted to be mobile-friendly.

That means, making sure that your website is mobile-friendly. Make sure your sales page is mobile-friendly. And most of all, make sure that your landing pages are mobile-friendly.

People you market to on Instagram are going to come into contact with your websites and landing pages via the mobile route.

So, you had better be ready! If you have a website that isn't mobile-friendly and they come across as a tiny, hard-to-read webpage, they are going to get frustrated and blow it off. Of course, that is not what you want happening!

Think Quick and to the Point

One of the things we are going to be emphasizing is that you need to be right on point at all times. The thing to keep in mind is something we have already mentioned before – on mobile, people have the attention span of a gnat. So you need to grab people's attention immediately, whether it's in your posts, your videos, or on your bio. You are going to use your bio as a gateway to your landing pages, so you got to make sure the bio gets its point across quickly.

Summing Up

Instagram is deceptively simple. When I first tried out the app a while back, my first reaction was, *OK, that's cute but so what?*

Gasoline On Fire

I missed the point entirely. The simplicity of Instagram is also its strength. It's a huge profit machine, provided that you set up your business presence on the app just right. Even more to the point is that it's cheap. If you spend any money at all – and frankly if you are the patient type who can afford to wait – you can get by without spending, it's going to be massively low-cost. Remember that everything is relative, but if you tried running Google PPC or Facebook ads, you would have to spend a lot more money.

So, look at the advantages: Low cost of entry, simplicity, and massive audiences to reach.

On a dollar-per-customer basis, Instagram comes out tops or near the top.

One last point to consider: Remember that, fundamentally, human beings are visual creatures.

Gasoline On Fire

And that is why Instagram is such a strong platform. It's a platform that is based on human nature in the sense that photographs are totally visual – you see something beautiful in a pic and you are IMMEDIATELY taken in.

So, when we're posting on Instagram, the goal is to evoke an instant reaction. We aren't going to be using a lot of the tools that are normally used in online marketing – many of you will find that a relief.

For example, a long-form sales letter has no place on Instagram. So, you don't have to spend hours agonizing over making a new sales letter, going over every word to make sure that's its just right and not something that will cause people to lose attention.

You also don't have to make long video presentations. That will save you a lot of trouble too, and you won't need to bother with fancy preparation and presentations that such videos may require. You're also not going to have to bother with hiring a slick-sounding announcer either.

So, not having to deal with those long-form methods of sales pitching can definitely make things quite a bit simpler.

But with that said, remember that your posts have to be spot on. So, you're going to have to *perfect* making a single image that directly speaks to a lot of people. If you make an Instagram story, it's only going to be 15-seconds long – quite a bit different than making a 12-minute video sales letter.

Of course, a successful business uses multiple platforms. I'm certainly not saying that you should go exclusive Instagram, but it does provide a great platform for you to drive customers towards your business. Now, let's look at how to create an account and the issues associated with that.

Chapter 2: Creating an Instagram Account

Now, we are going to talk about account creation. When you're setting up your Instagram account, the mere act of setting up the account is going to be one of the most important things that you can do. It's important to plan ahead and get it right before you get going. If you start running your Instagram account and then later decide that you want to change your name and so forth, all that's going to do is create problems. The bottom line is that, if you make changes later after you've already got followers, you're probably going to end up losing followers. So, why not get it right from the beginning?

Choosing a Name

Gasoline On Fire

Before you sign up on Instagram, the first thing you should do is choose a name that you're planning to use as your user name. Now, it may turn out that you have to make minor modifications, but the important thing to do is to have a name that is consistent across your entire web presence. So, what we're looking at here is that you want to have a meaningful Instagram account name that is easily recognizable, and we want to have that same name used on your email address as well as on your website domain. So, if you already have an existing business and the name really isn't suitable for Instagram, it might be good to create a separate website just for the purposes of marketing on Instagram. Keep in mind that you also have to have a lead page or "squeeze pages", as some people call it, and you're going to want to have that tied to your domain name as well. I like to use ClickFunnels for my squeeze pages – quite frankly hands-down, it's the best out there. A good thing about ClickFunnels - well there are a lot of good things about it - but one thing that I like about it, especially, is the ability to preview the mobile version while you're building it. Anyway, we are getting ahead of ourselves because creating the final draft and everything, is something we're going to look at down the road here.

So, just a few notes about the name of your Instagram account: The first thing to keep in mind is that people are going to want to use your name for searches. We're also considering people that are not your followers, so you want your name to be expressive and descriptive for the niche that you are marketing to. So although you might be tempted to choose a name that is very creative but doesn't immediately call to mind the targeted niche, or the purpose of your business, that's probably not the best name to use.

And, of course, you're also going to want to watch out for copyright infringement and those types of issues.

Gasoline On Fire

OK, so to summarize, you don't want to get tangled up in copyright infringement, obviously. Second, you want a name that makes sense immediately. Remember that on Instagram, everything is nearly instantaneous. So, your name should communicate your niche and/or the purpose of your business instantly.

Using your personal name for your Instagram account name is a bad idea. So, to give an idea of what we're talking about here, suppose that Mary Jones owns an art gallery. So, she wants to create an Instagram account to show potential buyers some of the paintings in her gallery that are available for sale. She might be naïve, or she might just be anxious, and so she goes immediately to Instagram and simply opens an account using her personal name as the Instagram username. Or for the sake of use, she might log into Instagram with her Facebook account. She would be better off using "ModernArtGallery" as her username (or whatever style of art that she is advertising, as the case may be) instead.

But the key lesson for us marketers is to prepare all of this ahead of time. So the exact phrase "modern art gallery" may not even be available, but it wouldn't be too hard to make some type of derivative of it. But, let's say, for the sake of argument, that it is available. So, before Mary goes to create her Instagram account, she should buy a domain name where she's going to put her landing page and so forth. Following that, let's say she manages to get modernartgallery.com, then she can create an email address associated with the website, such as Mary.Jones@modernartgallery.com. You can display your email address on Instagram, so we want all your accounts to use that same phrase so that the business is branded on Instagram. The name "ModernArtGallery" clearly communicates what the business is about. It's easy to remember, and it's also got words in it that people who haven't seen Mary's page yet, but are interested in her niche, are going to be searching for.

You should also use the same phrase not only for the domain name and email address, but also to create a Facebook page. Although the ideal situation is to aim to get free traffic, at some point, you might want to advertise on Facebook, and you can advertise through Facebook Advertising on Instagram and Facebook all at the same time.

It might also be advisable for our imaginary friend Mary Jones to create a blog related to her art gallery and also call it by the same name.

I am sure you get the idea. You want to settle on a phrase that is descriptive of your niche and immediately searchable, and use that for your

Instagram name as well, to tie across your entire web presence. Keep in mind that you can use periods and underscores in Instagram names. So, for example, if the phrase we want to use is not available as a username, we could use something like "Modern.Art.Gallery." for the username. Alternatively, we could use "modern_art_gallery". Obviously, these are not nearly as attractive as the original phrase.

There are other ways we could settle on the desired name – for example, if Mary's gallery was located in Glendale, maybe she can use "GlendaleArts", instead.

Your username is going to impact how you show up in search results, so you aren't going to want to use common phrases that are more generic and more popular. This is the same as thinking about pay-per-click (PPC) advertising – you probably want to use long-tail keywords for more traffic, rather than trying to compete for something that everyone is using.

Why is Domain Name Important?

Keep in mind that, besides branding, you can feature your domain name in your Instagram bio. You'll want everything to be consistent and easy to remember.

Why Do You Want an Instagram Account?

Another thing to consider before you open the Instagram account is that you need to have a clear idea as to why you want to open the account. So, for example, if you are an affiliate marketer, and you are going to be marketing multiple products off of Clickbank, you probably want a different Instagram account for each niche. So, for example, if I was a Clickbank affiliate and I was selling a ketogenic diet product, but I was also selling a Biz Opp or a make-money-online product, I would not want to mix those two very different items into one Instagram account. On the other hand, if I made a generic weight loss account, it would be more reasonable to promote different types of diets on the same account. So, if I browse Clickbank, it's pretty easy to find multiple ketogenic diet products. I could go either way on this one, because people that are into the ketogenic diet are probably also going to be interested in multiple weight-loss methods.

So, I searched and found a product called the "red tea detox". that claims it can help with weight loss. So, you could promote that and a ketogenic diet product through the same Instagram account. But if you're using your Instagram account to promote a Forex product, it's probably not reasonable to promote the red tea detox product on the same Instagram account. Now, I know that sounds obvious, but the reality is that far too many people don't think these things through ahead of time.

So, let's get back to the main point for the section: You want to have a clear idea about the main purpose of the Instagram account. If something doesn't contribute to the main purpose of the Instagram account, then that something should be promoted on a different Instagram account.

Types of Instagram Accounts

So, the purpose of the Instagram account is also going to influence the type of account that you will use. It turns out that there are actually multiple options of Instagram accounts that can be opened. The most basic division is that you can open a personal Instagram account or a business Instagram account.

There is also another option called a "niche" or "feature" account. This is very useful if you are aiming at a specific niche or topic. So, rather than being focused on an individual or business like a traditional Instagram account, a feature account is a topic-based account.

You can use the account to provide tips for users, and frankly, this fits right in with many affiliate-marketing products. So, to use an example, suppose that you sell health guides for the care of kittens. You could create an Instagram account that is in the niche of kittens. Then, you could focus on posting tips and advice related to keeping the kittens healthy, such as: What they eat, vet visits, and so forth.

A niche or feature account can help you remain disciplined and focused. One of the mistakes people make on Instagram is that they create a personal account and try to build up followers, and then bombard their followers with random information. That is not something that's going to be successful in maintaining your followers and driving buyers to your business.

Using a feature account or "niche account", as some people call them, you are forced to keep things focused on one specific area. So, you could, for example, create a feature account on the ketogenic diet, even if you were selling multiple weight-loss products. But on that one feature account, you could build an audience that is specifically interested in the ketogenic diet and you could routinely share tips about it with them, and that would build the loyalty of your followers. If you were also marketing affiliate offers from Clickbank for making money with an online business, you could also have a feature account for that. That is going to be way more effective than creating a personal Instagram account, sometimes posting about earning money with your online business, and then the following day posting about the ketogenic diet.

Another idea for a feature account: You can use it to post advice from famous experts in your field. That will help drive traffic and followers to your account. Moreover, as you add followers to your feature account, other people who are also interested in promoting on Instagram may want to post something on your account. This, of course, would be a sales opportunity for you. You can charge them for the privilege.

Of course, a great way to use the account would be to link to your website with the offer in your bio.

Chapter 3: Unwritten Rules of Instagram

Instagram is a social network after all, and so it has social rules that apply when you're participating in it, even if they aren't stated upfront. As a business, or using an account for business purposes, you're going to have some extra rules you should observe, and also some rules for personal users that don't apply to you.

Post Often, But Don't Post Too Often

Posting on Instagram is going to involve a balance between spamming and ghosting. In the early phases of your account, you are probably going to want to post 2-3 times per day in order to generate growth. Over the long term, a good rule of thumb is to post once per day. You are not going to want people to feel overburdened by your posting. Seeing it too much, they might get sick of you or feel that you are pushy, and you might lose followers. On the other hand, if you don't post enough, you might find yourself losing followers as well. Not posting frequently can lead to a situation where you become irrelevant.

Posting During Peak Times

You'll have to figure out what are the best times to post for your particular business and audience. But always keep in mind the short attention spans and fast movement of the platform. So, you want to post at peak times to get the maximum audiences' attention.

Don't Post on Friday/Saturday Nights

Whether people are out on the town or at home sitting on the couch for a Netflix binge, you don't want to be trying to contact your followers during times when you know that their focus is probably not going to be on your business, or even on Instagram.

As a Business Poster, Focus on Quality

While you do need to post at a certain level to drive traffic, you need to post quality information. Don't force yourself to put something up even when you really don't have something to offer. If you post for the sake of posting and it's not high-quality information or a good image, people are going to think you're cheap and you might lose followers.

Don't Make it personal, Unless YOU are the Brand

If you're selling a product, people don't care about you, as it relates to the product. That's why you should set up a business account and maybe one or more feature accounts. Don't make yourself the focus – that is, unless you are also the brand. Take Frank Kern, for example (if you aren't familiar with him, Google to find out). In this case, Frank Kern IS the brand, so a "Frank Kern" account makes sense, and even personal posts from Frank Kern make sense. But if you are not a personal coach like that, then keep yourself out of it most of the time.

Minimize Selfies

Selfies are overdone. One or two are fine, but don't make it a regular thing.

Use Analytics

Business accounts have access to post analytics, so you can find out when you should post and other information using analytics.

Be Authentic

Believe it or not, even through a computer screen or on a mobile phone, people can tell when you're not genuine. So, if you are going to try and pitch a product you aren't very enthusiastic about, you might reconsider and find something else that actually syncs with your passions.

Engage

Post a comment that asks a question. You want to engage your prospects. You also want to build trust. Asking questions helps people to realize that you are a real person, and this will help them trust you later if you are recommending a product to them.

Don't Buy Likes

One time, I ran an iPhone app business. An acquaintance was always buying reviews for his apps. It struck me as completely cheesy. The reviews were naturally all 5-star, and all obviously fake. Buying followers is also a no-no. Instagram could ban your account if they find out you've done either, but even if they don't, having fake followers or likes isn't going to be beneficial. Success in business starts with being genuine.

Add Value

Make sure that you add value to people's lives. If you are running a feature account, add valuable tips. Adding value ensures that your business will succeed and grow.

Don't Overdo filters

Keep your photos clean and natural. Some use of filters is obviously acceptable, but if you overdo it, you're going to turn people off.

Don't Post Multiple Photos in a Row

Doing so has a spammy effect that will lead to you lose followers.

Be Judicious About Following People

Part of your goal with a business-oriented account is establishing yourself as an authority figure. If you are following more people than are following you, it doesn't give that impression. You should aim to have more followers than the number that you are following.

Don't Post Collages

Keep your photos simple – one image, one message. Don't post collages – you don't want people having to struggle to see what's on their phone.

Avoid Overused Quotes and Clichés

It's too easy to post yet another Churchill quote, but don't do it. Posting something that people have heard a hundred times before isn't going to help you get followers.

Post Actionable Tips

If you are trying to grow your business and establish yourself as an authority figure, post tips and tricks people can use and apply immediately. This will help reinforce the idea that you are providing value to your prospects.

Be Careful With the Hashtags

Too many hashtags look cheesy and make it look like you're a little desperate for attention.

Avoid Putting "#nofilter"

If you know what I mean. Just don't. It puts people off.

Chapter 4: Your logo = Your Hook

Believe it or not, your logo is one of the most important aspects of creating your Instagram account. This is nothing new – think about how much work has gone into creating logos for major corporations: The McDonald's golden arches or the logo for Pepsi or BMW. If you are going to be building a brand, even though you're not going to be reaching the same tens of millions of people that major brands do, your logo is going to be important. It helps uniquely position your business on Instagram and helps make you instantly recognizable.

A logo helps people recognize your posts

When your posts show up in a newsfeed, you want your followers to be able to recognize you immediately. You can do this with a good, memorable, yet simple logo.

Use contrast when designing your logo

The goal with a logo is instant recognition. Think Starbucks or Audi. On a smartphone, your logo is going to be relatively small. So, it needs to stand out. Think about comfortable but contrasting colors. A good example here is a black background with a white logo, or vice versa. That is just an example – we are not saying you should actually use black & white. Make sure the colors that you do choose contrast but are also in harmony. There are some colors that contrast too sharply and thus look harsh.

Settle on core colors for a brand

You can use core colors for your brand. Notice that many large companies do this, i.e., the color schemes used by various soft drinks companies. The logo can reinforce the colors used, and you can use the same colors in the text on your images or as background colors. This reinforcement helps build brand identity.

Have a professional design your logo

It's not good to look amateurish. There are so many inexpensive designers for digital assets that there is no excuse for you to be designing your own logo. A good place to look for a designer is on Fiverr. Find a designer who has a lot of good examples of past work. Then work with them closely, letting them know what you want to communicate with the logo. Also, let them know that you need the logo to look good but also stand out even when displayed as a small image. You should also look for designers who have experience specifically related to Instagram.

Chapter 5: Call-to-Action in Your Bio

Later in the book, we are going to talk about sales funnels. The purpose of a sales funnel is to collect leads. People who know about internet marketing know that in order to close a sale online, you have to do some preselling. In short, the purpose of your Instagram account, aside from bringing traffic and leads, is to presell those leads. That is why it's doubly important that you add value with your Instagram account by providing followers with valuable information. The link between you and your followers on the Instagram account will also satisfy the purpose of building trust and authority if you handle your posts correctly. So, if someone has been following you on Instagram and enjoying your posts, they already trust you, and they are going to be interested when you recommend a product or service to them.

For this reason, Instagram can be a good addition to your strategy as an online marketer.

Connect your Bio to your Sales Funnel/Website

The point of contact between your website and Instagram account is going to be through your bio. It is here where you can include a link to your sales funnel pages.

Like everything else on Instagram, there is not much room here for long amounts of text. In order to communicate the most information in the least amount of space, it is recommended that you use a list of bullet points to quickly communicate to your followers what your Instagram brand is all about.

Explain your Brand

In your bio, you can have a set of bullet points in a list that explains the whats, whys, and hows of your offerings. Remember, space is limited, so these have to be quick and to the point. You are not hoping to close the sale right then and there – all you are hoping for is to get them to click on your link, so it's not important to have a huge sales pitch here. They click on the link and then they are taken to your landing page.

Let your prospects know why you have an Instagram account and why you are offering the product that you are offering. Keep in mind, however, that we are going to use a landing page and we're going to be offering your followers a free gift, so it's not necessary to sell them the product at this point. We only want to entice them enough to tap on the link to your website.

Action Buttons

Last year, Instagram began rolling out action buttons that could be used on business accounts. Unfortunately, they are extremely limited, and while they started with just four buttons, only three are currently available. They allow the follower to order food through a restaurant, reserve seats at a restaurant, or buy tickets to an event.

It would be nice if they had a button that would take followers to your website, but unfortunately, the buttons described above are the only ones available at this time. It's pretty amazing that functions are still so limited with this, even though it's been nearly a year since the buttons were first introduced.

So, unless you have a restaurant, the action buttons are completely useless at this time.

Limited Space

Instagram bios only allow 150 characters. So, there isn't much you can say here, and so you should get to the point right away. Note that some of the information we are discussing here, like your URL, does not count toward the 150 character limit.

Items to Communicate With

Your Instagram bio can be thought of as a landing page of its own. In fact, in the Instagram universe, it's often going to play that sort of role. Many users will be seeing your profile for the very first time when they come to your bio, having come to it from possibly seeing one of your posts, or by tapping on a hashtag.

At the very least, you'll want to grab this new lead. You can't collect emails directly on Instagram, so your bio has to effectively communicate to someone why they should follow you. In order to write a good copy here, put yourself in their shoes and imagine yourself arriving on the page for the first time, not knowing whom the page represents or what the business is about.

Then think about what you could say to that person that would, at a minimum, compel them to follow your account, so that at least you'll have future opportunities to communicate with that particular lead. Secondly, hopefully, you can get a lot of the people who look at your bio to click on your website link.

But I can't emphasize how important it is to get a "follow". If someone clicks on the website link, oftentimes, they are going to be interested in your offer, but they might not be compelled to sign up for your email list the first time they visit the page. If you are familiar with Facebook advertising, then you know how re-targeting works. I like to think of grabbing followers as a method of retargeting, and it doesn't cost a penny. If you can get the prospect to follow you on Instagram, then you have a hold of them for future communication. You can possibly convince them through a post or a future visit to your bio again to go ahead and sign up for your email list.

Include a Keyword

One trick some businesses use is to include a keyword in your Instagram name. So, if you are a fitness guru named "ACME", who is trying affiliate marketing for a ketogenic diet guide, you could actually list your Instagram business name as "ACME Ketogenic Diet".

Keep in mind that you will have a Name and a Username. The username is your Instagram handle, like "@ModernArtGallery".

Website

The website entry on your bio is the only place where Instagram currently allows clickable links. So, this is where you are going to put the link to your landing page.

Category

Your Instagram bio, if you have a business account, will have a category. You can use this to further communicate to prospects what your business is all about.

Contact Information

Instagram also allows you to include contact information for your business. This can include a physical address or email address. The contact information does not count toward the 150 character limit, so some clever businesses actually put more descriptive information here rather than actual information about their contact info.

Using Downward-Pointing Fingers

Many people include a downward-pointing finger emoji in their bio. The reason this is done is because the clickable link that you can include in your bio appears immediately below the 150 characters of text.

Chapter 6: Modeling The Success of Others

When building your online and Instagram business, there is no sense in reinventing the wheel. That doesn't mean you COPY other people exactly – you model it. Before you actually create your Instagram business account, create a personal account for browsing purposes. Your goal of using this account will be to spy on competitors or real big players in your market niche. You want to follow them and see what they are doing, right through that link on their bio.

Find Key Players in Your Niche

The first step is to search and find key players in your niche. You want to look for people that have a large following. Now, it's impossible to give specific numbers for this, unfortunately, because the sizes of different markets are very different. For example, let's consider two animal-related markets: Dog owners and horse owners. There are probably 5 - 10 dog owners in the United States for every horse owner. So, you can't make an apples-and-oranges comparison. If you are selling a horse-training product, you're not going to be able to gauge the success rate by number of followers from looking at people selling dog-training products. They may have millions of followers, but a successful horse trainer on Instagram may only have 110,000 followers.

So, you want to find the most successful accounts in your niche, and then follow them.

Visit Their Bio

The first thing to do is to visit the bio. Pay attention to keywords and most importantly, any hashtags used. One thing you will want to copy is hashtags that successful people in your niche are using to get noticed.

Then write down their bio – here we are talking about the 150-character description. The important thing here isn't to write down the bio to copy it, but rather, to note down the key points that they get across in their bio. So when you read it, analyze the bio and write down key features andor benefits they cite in their bio. Once you have identified the key points, you may want to use those to build your own bio around them.

Click on the Website

You should always click on the website of a successful Instagram business account in your niche and find out what kind of website they take their users to. You may or may not want to follow their example on this one. If they are the vendor of a Clickbank account, they might take visitors to their sales page. As an affiliate, that is not the best course of action for you. You will always need to take visitors to a landing page instead.

Keep an Eye on Their Posts and Stories

You'll also want to closely monitor the posts that they put up along with any stories. Write down the text used in any images, and note their colors and fonts. Also, pay attention to any hashtags they are using on their posts. If they have a large number of followers for your niche, then they know what hashtags work the best to get eyeballs.

Another thing to look at is any preferred color schemes, if any, that they are using in their posts or their logos. This might sound strange, but having the right color schemes for your niche can be helpful in some cases.

Chapter 7: The Basics of a Sales Funnel

If you are involved in internet marketing but don't know what a sales funnel is, then you must be living under a rock. In the old days of Internet marketing, it was possible to run pay-per-click (PPC) ads that simply took the viewer from the ad right to a sales page. Those were the good old days. Back then, people just weren't all that sophisticated about the Internet and Internet marketing. It was all brand new, and so was far easier to get people to click on ads to buy products.

The Gold Rush Days of Internet Marketing

Over time, those old methods began to lose their magic. As Internet users became more sophisticated, it became more and more important to pre-sell prospects. However, there was another development: Marketers began to realize that if they could grab the email address of someone, that they would be able to get them to buy a product that they would not normally buy on just one exposure.

So, this shouldn't be too surprising – let's say that you have an interest in buying a new car. Are you going to rush out and buy the very first car that you see? Okay, yes, I know that in some cases, that's exactly what's going to happen. But let's say that those people are not the keenest people on the block. So what happens is, instead of rushing out and buying a car, you go out and you casually look at cars for a while. You may do this for an extended period of time before you actually make up your mind what type of car you want, and whether or not you're actually going to buy a car.

This process of browsing around and thinking about it for a while isn't just happening with the expensive ticket items like cars. People do this with all sorts of things like shoes, clothing, or even cell phones. People certainly do it for computers. They might even do it at the grocery store.

Getting Back in Contact with Prospects

So, on the Internet, people are doing this, too. Let's say you have the greatest sales page ever written. We all know that cold traffic isn't going to convert all that well on even the best sales page. But you might get a few percentage of your users visiting the sales page and buying it. But what about all those people that have left? So let's say that your sales page - the greatest one that was ever written - converts about 5% of visitors.

100 people visit the site, 5 of them by your product, so you make some money. But those other 95 people

left and they will never be heard from again. You might be satisfied with the 5 sales, but you're leaving a lot of money on the table. Those 95 people that left are not simply people that just left and are never going to buy. In fact, although they didn't buy, many of those folks were probably very interested in the product. So, it becomes a question of *if only we could talk to them again, we could easily get them to buy the offer.*

But the Internet isn't necessarily a place where people are going to be able to come back again to some obscure webpage. With this in mind, Internet marketers began to wonder how they could get back in contact with those people – many of whom would probably buy the product, but weren't hundred percent convinced the first time they visited the website. Who knows what their reason could be? Maybe some people are visiting the website on Monday, and the product costs, say, $97, but they don't get paid until the following Friday and so they can't afford it. But if you could get in touch with them later after they got paid, they would probably go ahead and buy it.

Other people may simply be more skeptical. So, the first time they see the site, they're kind of intrigued, but they aren't ready to pull out their credit card. The thing about people like that is that even a little bit of talking can't push them over the edge so that they do end up buying the product.

Okay, so we are going to be able to consider every single little reason that someone may or may not buy a product the first time they visit your website. The point is, there are a lot of people who are interested, but aren't going to buy on the first exposure. So, all we need is some other way to get in contact with them later. And this is where the idea of collecting emails from website visitors was born. You could think of it as a kind of Internet business card – we're getting someone's phone number. A lot of people who go shopping, say, at some furniture store, for example – they go in and browse, and then they leave. The salesman can just let them leave, or if he is smart, he is going to get their number and give them his business card. That way, when they're "thinking about it", he can sell them the sofa, or whatever they were looking at in the future.

Sidebars and Popups

Okay, so after this concept came about, many people began designing websites that had sidebars where people could enter their email address. People figured out that you could get someone's email address if you offered them something of value in exchange. You could either write a short book or make a video training course, or something like that. But the point is: You offer it for free. Let's say we are talking about the stock market niche. So, on your stock market website, you have a sidebar that says, "Free report reveals the secrets used by insider traders". Then you would have a call-to-action button below the form where people could enter their name and email address. The button might say something like, "Yes! Send me the free report".

In this case, you're hoping that the person will be visiting your website where you probably have a lot of content of interest. So maybe they are reading an article; any hope that they're going to notice that sidebar?

But of course, a huge fraction of these visitors to your website will simply be going to ignore the sidebar. So, what to do next? Well, of course, Internet marketers figured that out right away. They invented the annoying pop-ups. So, when you open a webpage, maybe after a one-or-three-second delay, a pop-up appears on the screen asking for your email address. I don't know about you, but I find that extremely annoying. Despite this, these types of pop-ups are still used with amazing frequency. It seems like you can hardly visit the website without them trying to grab your email address. And there's a reason that they're trying to do that. The simple fact is that, once you've got someone's email address, the theory that they will buy in future works. So let's get back to the topic at hand and see how things develop. Although those pop-ups are quite annoying, there has to be a better way to capture their contact information. Over time, this led to the concept of the "sales funnel".

The Landing Page

So, what markers wanted was an easy way to collect someone's email address. This led to the development of a single-page website. It really doesn't have to be a single-page website all by itself. It could, of course, be a single page on your bigger website. It really doesn't matter if you just want to have a destination whose sole purpose is to collect someone's email address in exchange for a free giveaway of some kind.

So, gone are the days of the long sales letter. Well, actually, what we're going to find out is that it was buried in a secret location. But instead of sending cold sales letters to the prospects, the way things will be done is to have a single and very simple page with a sign-up form and an offer for a free report, video or something else in exchange for their email address.

Sales Funnel Steps

So, this brings us to the concept of the "sales funnel". What you want to do is, you want to grab the prospect that's at the top of the funnel. So, you want them to enter the funnel and go all the way down until they pass out of the funnel, which is symbolic of the client actually buying the product. The landing page is the first step where you get the client into the funnel. So, when they sign up to join your email list, they are in the funnel.

Once a prospect is in the funnel, then you're free to advertise to them, but of course, we are going to do it in a subtle fashion. The way this is done is by using emails to communicate with them. We will talk about emails more in the last chapter. So, right now, the details are not that important.

So, you can do two things: The first step is that, when someone signs up for your email list, you take them to a second webpage. This is sometimes known as the "thank you" page. So you can put on this new webpage "Thank you for signing up for the newsletter!" Or something like that. On the thank you page, you give the prospect the actual free products that you had promised them. You can also include a link or, hopefully, a big "call-to-action" button on the thank you page, which would take them directly to the sales page. That may or may not work sometimes, but it doesn't matter, because we have their email address now, and we can contact them whenever we want to. So, assuming that you're not crazy and your free giveaway is directly related to what you're selling, the giveaway product is going to help convince them that they should buy the actual product. Earlier, we were talking about selling a car; you can think of the free giveaway as a type of test drive. So, you actually want to put your best foot forward in that free giveaway. Don't just throw something sloppily together for the sake of doing so. The free giveaway is a very important opportunity to convince the prospect that you offer quality products that are going to help them solve whatever problem your product claims to solve. So, you give them a free guide or something, and then inside the free guide, you put plenty of links to the actual sales page. At that point, people may or may not still buy the product. But, over time, you're going to send them emails with valuable information about the same product for the issues that it solves, and with each email, you add value. The more value that you add, the more likely that you're going to close sales.

In many cases, people will try to sell using a webinar. This is an online event where people visit, and you give them some sort of presentation that may last an hour or so in order to help sell the product. The higher the price of the products, the more useful the webinar will be. So, what some people will do is, they have their "thank you" page set up as a webinar registration page. So, then the prospect will get an email a few days later announcing the webinar. In that model, the webinar itself is the sales pitch, although there could be a follow-up later.

The Sales Page

A funnel is going to have multiple steps. As we described, the very top step is the landing page.

Maybe, right below that, you have the person entering the funnel, so, the second step would be the thank you page for signing up and the person joining the email list. The next stage after that further down the funnel would be the sales page. People nowadays are still using traditional sales pages. In fact, they've been using sales pages for decades, if not longer. In the old days, people use and actually write a letter in this format. That's why we have those long sales pages now – they are simply a computer adaptation of what people have been doing since the 1920s, or even before that. So, sales pages aren't going anywhere. They've just been buried in a secret location. You use your funnel to guide the prospect to that secret location.

Now many people are going to be harder to sell to than others, so as you'll see, we can use an email list to keep selling to them and sending them back to the sales page. So, you're going to repeatedly send them emails, and the emails will contain links to the sales page. Also, the free book that you gave them is going to have links from the book to the sales page. So, whoever signs up for your list is going to be repeatedly bombarded by the sales page. And frankly, that's what it takes in a lot of cases to get people to buy things. But it works, and so that's why people do it.

The simplest type of funnel simply goes from landing page to thank you page, to a sales page, and then there is a second thank you page that is used if someone actually buys the product.

Depending on the complexity of your offer, the funnel can end there.

Upsells and downsells

Many people, however, don't let it end there, and they have more steps in the funnel. So, the thank you page, if the funnel ends at the sales page, would have access to the actual product. But, we may, instead, offer upsells to the customer. So, for example, let's say that I'm selling a ketogenic diet guide. Let's say the guide cost $47. So, the person gets convinced and they go through and buy it. But after they click the "purchase" button, you say *wait a minute*. Then you offer them a chance for a more expensive product that has more benefits. So in this particular example, I could say something like you have a one-time chance to sign up for a customize keto diet plan that will be developed for your exact body type, weight, age, and gender. That might cost, say, $97. You can see that such a product would be beneficial, so many of the people who bought the first product are going to buy that product that's also offered in the funnel.

So, you can add even more steps. Let's say that's someone declines to buy the $97 custom plan. Then you could offer a downsell at that point, which would be another step in your funnel. So, just to continue my example, I could offer them a $27 ketogenic cookbook.

If you wanted to make it more complicated and have more chances to make money on the backend, then you could have the very expensive product offered after they buy the customized plan. So, maybe you could say, "Upgrade your customized plan for $199 and we will deliver you a month's worth of pre-made keto meals."

So, that's probably a good idea. Maybe some of you out there will start a business selling ketogenic meal plans. But the only point of this exercise was to illustrate what a sales funnel is.

Connecting to Instagram

One of the advantages that we have in the case of using Instagram is that we have warmed up our sales prospects using Instagram accounts. So, let's go ahead and continue with the previous example. My sales funnel is set up to sell all those ketogenic diet products. So, what am I doing on Instagram about this? Well, I would have a feature or niche Instagram accounts that were focused on the ketogenic diet. Maybe, you could portray yourself as an expert on the diet. So, you would continually post advice and facts about the ketogenic diet.

So, if someone has been following you, they are going to be seeing all these information-filled posts. And obviously, they are not going to be following you unless they're interested in the ketogenic diet in the first place. But, over time, as they're seeing your posts, they would have grown to trust your knowledge about the diet. So, this is a very warm prospect as compared to what you normally get in Internet marketing. If you have a client like that and they are able to see your Instagram bio, and your 150-

word pitch is worded correctly, they're probably going to click on your link.

Then, as they click on the link, they will see that you're offering some type of free report related to the ketogenic diet. Now, since they already know you, and you have already convinced them that you're credible through your Instagram posts on your feature account that are providing them tips and tricks related to the ketogenic diet, you are going to have a huge conversion rate of people signing up for the newsletter. People already familiar with your postings on the Instagram account will gladly give you their email address in exchange for the free reports that you've written.

The good thing about this is that your Instagram account has cost you virtually nothing. The only thing that it has cost you are a few minutes of time each day designing your posts and possibly doing things like reaching out to other people in your niche and taking steps to try and grow your following.

So, the bottom line is that it's one of the best business models around. I honestly can't think of another way where you already have people warmed up, and already trusting you as an expert before they even get to the landing page itself. For the vast majority of Internet businesses, the landing page is going to be a place where cold prospects appear. The case of a celebrity who has an online business might be a good illustration for this, however. Since people already know the celebrity (of course, they don't actually know them – but you understand what I mean), they would already be pretty warmed up to sign up for a newsletter on offer from the celebrity on the get-go.

So, that is how you can use a sales funnel in conjunction with your Instagram account. You go to your bio and the link in your bio should be set to the landing page – that would be the entry point of the sales funnel.

Chapter 8: Generating Content

If you don't have good content that you're posting on Instagram, your sales funnel is going to be completely useless. You need to be building an audience of engaged followers so that you're getting a steady stream of people looking at your bio, with some of them clicking on the link. You probably already know that you post photos on Instagram, but you can also post short videos, called "Stories", as well as creating engagement groups. Let's go ahead and talk about building your following on Instagram by generating content.

The Best Ways to Post Photos

Posting relevant, high-quality content is going to be the lifeblood of your Instagram sales funnel. You are going to want to post 2 - 3 times per day while growing your Instagram following, but you don't want to just post for the sake of posting. You want to have a solid message for your audience, and you want that message displayed in a way that doesn't look amateurish. You can leverage on several apps to make your images look great, and also include your logo on your posts so that you can keep building your brand.

When building a business on Instagram, one thing you want to do is to be consistent in the style of your content. If you decide to create multiple feature accounts, each account can have its own style. Just be consistent within the account. Think about a major brand like Starbucks. If they constantly changed their color schemes and designs, it would be confusing and look like they were poorly managed. So, pick a style you are going to use for your account, and stick with it.

Which app you use - and there are many to choose from - will depend, in part, on how deeply you want to get into designing your photos. If you are big on design, then **Adobe Post** could be the app you are looking for. It's more sophisticated than others and allows you to do more. If you are an Adobe person already, using Photoshop and Illustrator, then Adobe Post might be suitable for you. For most people though, it's going to be too much. The bottom line with Adobe Post is if you are already very comfortable with Photoshop and Illustrator, it might be a solid option for you. If you are not, it might involve having to put time into learning the app, and that may be time better spent on other activities. The reason is there are simpler apps out there which will be able to do everything you need.

Something to keep in mind is that you want to operate with as much efficiency as possible. Remember that Instagram can be described by the word "rapid". You want to get things done as quickly as possible on Instagram so that you can post 3 times a day, but you are going to need to allocate time throughout the day to work on other aspects of your business. Whatever that might be - it could be building out your website, posting on a blog, or working on your sales funnel - your work on Instagram should be focused on getting to the core message you want to communicate quickly, getting a high-quality image, making the Instagram version of it, and posting as quickly as possible. You don't want to be spending hours on it that you could spend doing something else.

Canva is a good app that you can use to overlay text and make it look professional. One of the nice features about Canva is that it has templates you can use – a big help in speeding up your productivity. One nice feature of Canva is that it allows you to create Instagram Stories. It is a free download for your smartphone or tablet.

Gasoline On Fire

Word Swag is a great app to consider for use with Instagram. It's one of the most popular apps of this type on the App Store. On the Apple store, it has more than 61k ratings. Word Swag is simple to use and has the advantage of being able to take your picture right within the app to use as a background, or you can import an existing photo. A great feature of Word Swag, besides the amazing looking text you can overlay on your images, is the ability to include your logo in it.

Framematic can be used to make collage-style images. As we noted earlier, you want to avoid using collages. The reason is that you will want to quickly communicate a message with a business account, and too much going on in a collage can be distracting and difficult to see. There are some exceptions, if you keep the number of images in a collage limited. For example, people selling weight loss products might want to put "before" and "after" images in the same

Instagram post, and you could use Framematic to create a 2-image collage.

Square Sized can be a useful app to have on the side. It's designed to help get your apps Instagram-ready. You can add borders and text, alter colors, and add effects.

Another popular app for putting text on your photos is **Phonto**. It has many fonts available, and lets you do interesting things like erase part of the text, rotate the text, and so much more. You can include curved text and also select image themes.

Sprout Social can be a very useful app for business owners. This app isn't for creating images, but rather, it's an automation app for scheduling your postings ahead of time. So, you will be able to set up several images to post at specific times using this app. It also provides image-analytics information.

Royalty-Free Images

Don't think that you have to use your own photos all the time. In fact, for a business, it's perfectly OK to utilize high-quality stock images, provided that the images are completely congruent with your message and don't look too "plastic". While a lot of people want to look for stock photos that are free, it's more important to go for quality. If you cut corners in your business, then you aren't going to have long-term success.

I've used many different royalty-free photo sites in my business, but there are really only three that I recommend. Before I get to those, I will mention **Getty Images** which has a lot of very high-quality content, but it's also more expensive than the other sites (at least at the time of writing). I have found it to be too pricey to be worth any consideration.

The first site I'd recommend is **Dreamstime**. They have images in virtually every category, and depending on how many images you are going to use each month, they have some great deals to download unlimited monthly images.

Shutterstock is another good site. I have used Shutterstock to get short-video clips that were professionally done. You can buy by the image or get a monthly plan like Dreamstime.

A third option to look at which isn't quite as good but you can fit in most budgets is **DepositPhotos**. They have similar options for downloading individual images or using one of their monthly plans.

Don't be afraid to use stock photos. Most of your followers, and in many cases, probably all of your followers, are not running businesses and aren't even aware these sites exist. Stock photos can help you get professional level high-quality images that you might not have access to otherwise. For example, if you live in Iowa, you can use stock photo sites to get great shots of beach sunsets or of high-rise office buildings in New York City.

Apps for Instagram Stories

When you are running a business on Instagram, you certainly don't want to limit yourself to posting plain photos, even though that might be the mainstay of your activities. You also want to post Instagram stories. Some apps that might be useful for creating Instagram stories include **Videoshop**, which lets you shoot video right within the app, **Filmmaker Pro**, and **Adobe Spark Post**, which can be used to create animation effects using still photos. One advantage of Adobe Spark Post is that you can use it on your iOS or Android device and it also has a desktop version for those who want to get heavy into the design.

You can also consider some online video creators. **Magistro** is one site that is very popular for creating videos for Instagram Stories. It requires a subscription which is $4.99 a month. Another useful tool that you can use on the desktop is **Storrito**. When creating Instagram stories, since that can be a little more involved and you want it to be professional, many people prefer working from the Desktop.

Hiring Talent

Remember – you are in business to make money, and although it can be painful to spend upfront, people that take the money-saving attitude in business might end up finishing last. You need to put the best foot forward possible. With that in mind, if you are not the best design person, its better to spend a little money to get some high-quality content made that is going to help you build a following and get people going from Instagram to your sales funnel, than it is to post boring or cheap-looking imagery that has users saying "meh".

The good news is that you can find low-cost designers on Fiverr. You can save money because many people are using the site just to generate extra income, and you can also find many high-quality designers from "third world" countries that charge lower prices because the cost of living where they live is so much lower. The key to success taking this route is to avoid spending too much money on your first gig. First off, carefully evaluate the previous work claimed by the seller and check their reviews. You have to take this information with a grain of salt. However, Fiverr pushes people to leave reviews immediately after a job is turned in, and so people may have left reviews without carefully checking their results. Also, it's all too easy to swipe someone else's work and then claim it as your own. With that in mind, the best thing to do is to find someone you like and then have them do one standard job for you. Then you can see what they actually produce, and if it's not very good, you can find someone else and only put out a small amount of money. If they produced good work for you, then you can stick with them.

I don't recommend using hired talent to make regular posts for Instagram. You should get one of the apps discussed above, and you can make high-quality images yourself. When you might want to use hired talent, get someone with experience to make some Instagram stories for you. If you get high-quality Instagram stories that you can periodically post, this is going to go a very long way toward building a loyal following that is going to be ready to buy your products.

Repurposing

You can also repurpose images. That is, take the same original image and put a different message on it. This can save time, money, and hassle. The only advice for repurposing images is that you don't use the same image too many times and don't use it for a short time after you've posted the original. Wait a couple of weeks. When repurposing the image, focus on creating good content through your message that you overlay on the photo.

Writing Good Text

Having solid captions that are going to help sell your products is a key part of your posting. You don't want to be simply posting random messages. This can be hard for some people. Writing effective copy isn't easy to begin with, and with only one photo to work with, you've got to have your compelling copy written with a short amount of text.

You can use more text, but it will require a user to click on "More" to see it, so you either have to give them a strong reason to do so, or you have to accept that many people are going to not want to take that extra step. Any time in marketing where you can avoid adding extra actionable steps in, is preferred. That said, sometimes, you are still going to need to put more text.

The first piece of advice that I can give is to write a text that comes from your OWN heart. People like authenticity. That is going to win out over some cheesy sales letter every time. So yes, while you want to use traditional copywriting techniques that are known to drive sales, you also want to make sure that it's written in your authentic voice, and that it's genuine.

Use Questions

A good way to get people more engaged in your posts is to ask questions. This is also a technique that you can use in Facebook ads as well, if you are running them. A question prompts the viewer to think, and encourages them to engage with a post. The reason you would want to have a question at the top of a Facebook ad is to encourage the viewer to leave a comment. More comments mean more engagement and shares.

One time-tested way to ask a question is to say, "Who else wants…". For example:

Who else wants a dog that is well-behaved and doesn't chew up the couch again?

Another example:

Who else wants a dog that enjoys the backyard quietly, rather than constantly barking at every little sound?

People are in a kind of zombie-state while using their smartphones, and on Instagram, they are busy swiping. A question can act like a small shock that wakes up their brain and gets them to engage. When they are engaging, if you have the other parts of your post in place, then that is more likely to lead to clicks and signups on your sales funnel leads page.

List Features, Not Benefits

The best way to pre-sell someone and get them to click on your link is to focus on benefits. Don't list features. The feature-benefit dichotomy is one of the most difficult things for many people to master when it comes to marketing, but it's crucial to do so. Features are just facts about the product. So, if you were selling a sports car, a feature would be that it has a V-8 engine, and is red in color. A benefit would be describing how the buyer of the car would enjoy driving fast on the open highway.

Here is another example to help you understand the difference – let's consider a dog training product. A feature of the product might be:

Gasoline On Fire

Teach your dog to stop whining when you leave the room.

Features are important to disclose and you should list features on your sales pages, but benefits are more compelling, so take the front seat. Turning this into a benefit, we might say something like:

Sleep quietly every night as your dog enjoys their new home.

For another example, suppose that you were a car salesman selling a hybrid vehicle. A feature would be:

This car gets 45 mpg.

A benefit would be:

Save $3,492 a year on gasoline costs and spend less time at the pump.

So, before you even start posting on Instagram, get a notebook and start thinking of the product or products you are selling in terms of features and benefits. Then, write compelling messages that are short and to the point that tells the viewer what 2 of the benefits are.

Mention Your Free Giveaway

Remember that the hook for a sales funnel is to have a free giveaway of some kind that you offer the visitor in exchange for their email address? It's important to use the word FREE in your Instagram posts as well, because you want them to know they can get the free report, free video, or free webinar training – whatever you are offering. That is going to be important to increase the number of clicks that you get from Instagram.

Call-to-Action

One thing that beginners fail to do in marketing, in many cases, is to forget a call-to-action. A call-to-action is simply a link or button or descriptive text that tells the viewer what to do. So, you add your link with the words "CLICK HERE", or something to that effect. You will also want to take this message to heart on your sales pages on the web as well – make sure you ask customers to buy the product in multiple locations. Many beginning marketers are not explicit in what they want the user to do, and so lose many sales. The viewer needs you to tell them – they are not psychic.

Chapter 9: Working with Influencers

It should go without saying that the first step in working with influencers is to make sure that you have quality content. Before you contact an influencer, you need to make sure that your profile has a good amount of content already. It doesn't have to be a huge amount, but you want to make sure they don't make you look like a total beginner, either. So, let's say that before you contact your first influencer, you have around 25 posts already, and maybe 1 to 2 Instagram stories. You also want to make sure that you have everything set up on the back end. So, in that case, you'll have your sales funnel completely done up, and that includes having your email list ready and your autoresponder completely working. Make sure you test your sales funnel before you contact the influencers. Some problems of a technical nature might come up when you first build your sales funnel, so you want to make sure that you can visit the sales funnel, put in your email address, and actually receive the emails before you contact an influencer.

Now, when we talk about influencers, there can be different levels to consider. You can approach a lot of different people in your niche and you don't necessarily have to go for people with 1 million followers first. So, you can look for mid-range people to contact as well. The idea is simply to get people that are going to respond and be willing to help you. Close relevance to your topic of interest is also going to be important. In other words, it might be better to contact someone that only has 20,000 followers, whose topic is directly related to yours, than it would be to contact someone with 1 million followers whose focus is only tangentially related.

Buying a Post

Here's an interesting way to leverage on somebody else's followers list to help get followers to your own account and maybe even drive direct sales for direct visits to your landing page. First, what you want to do is to create a very good image with compelling copy for someone else to post on your behalf. So, when you post, you want to direct them back to your profile and your landing page URL. You can try this method with people with different numbers of followers. The number of followers that an Instagram account has is not the only metric you want to use. You also want to know their engagement rate. There is a tool online that you can use to put in an Instagram handle and get an estimate of their engagement rate. It's called **Phlanx**, and the link is right below:

https://phlanx.com/engagement-calculator

Gasoline On Fire

Decisions about whom to approach are going to be based on a combination of the number of followers and the engagement rate. For reference, on Instagram, the average engagement rate is about 3%. We can also look up some famous people to see what their engagement rates are. Kylie Jenner has an engagement rate of 4.7%. It's above the average, so pretty good. Beyonce is only at 2.47% – below average.

Now, even though a celebrity might have millions of followers, they aren't necessarily the best choice. You have to weigh many different factors. It could carry a huge amount of weight if a celebrity were to endorse your product. So, for a fantasy, we could imagine something like Kim Kardashian endorsing your ketogenic diet book. It would literally fly off the shelves. And that would be true even though she has a relatively low engagement rate.

However, one thing you want to take note of is not to look random in your postings. So, for that reason, at least most the time, you won't be looking at hitting a home run with a major influencer. Instead, what you want to do is go for mid-range accounts with decent numbers of followers that have high engagement rates, and as we mentioned earlier, that also have direct relevance to your product or service.

So, the first factor you want to look for is to make sure that they have an engagement rate that is above average. You can get an estimate of what their engagement is going to be by multiplying the engagement rate and the number of followers. If you can find engagement rates that are significantly higher than the average, those are good ones to select.

So, once you found your prospects, begin by following their account as an act of goodwill. After this, you can direct message them and propose that they post on your behalf and imagine that you'll provide the necessary information to go with the post. One way that this is done, which can help drive some traffic to you and also help you save money, is that you propose that they put up your post for a limited time period. So, you can try this approach: Find 3 to 5 Instagrammers in your niche that have follower counts ranging from between 20,000 and 100,000.

Then, you can direct message them and enquire about putting up your post on their account for a price range of $15-$300, depending on the number of followers they have. Vary your price offering according to the number of followers they have, and the engagement rate. So, for somebody with 20,000 followers and an average engagement rate, you might offer them $15 to put up your post for 12 hours. If an account has a high engagement rate and you are willing to offer more money, it's going to be worth it over the long term.

Another strategy when contacting them is to leave it open and let them tell you what their pricing is. You can even do some research on the account, including checking their bio to see if they actually are open to advertising other people's posts, and they may have the rates already listed somewhere. So, if they have a link to a website, be sure to check that out. If you're not going to mention a price, simply contact them with direct messaging and ask what it would cost to put up your post for a given amount of time period. You can have a range from 12 to 24 hours, and some may be willing to do it for more than a day, but that will cost more, obviously. A 12-hour range is actually a pretty good way to do it. One reason is that, chances are, they can post and cover their peak periods of engagement.

Direct Messaging

So, you're going to want to know how to do direct messaging inside Instagram in order to do this, but, of course, if they provide an email address, you can try that as well. But direct messaging is good because, often, people with large accounts are going to be getting a huge amount of email, and it might be hard to get in touch with them that way. I would use one method first, and if you don't hear back from them, try using the second method.

You can use direct messaging to send multiple things, including photos and posts. Don't send them the post or photo right away. When you send them a message, just enquire about paying them to put up your post later. Let them check out your profile on their own. This is another reason why you don't want to get too anxious when you're starting out and trying to contact influencers before your account is built out a little bit.

You're going to want to spend some time doing it the hard way with regular posting and building up some followers first. That way, when the influencer goes to look at your account, they can see that you're drawing followers and that you're posting quality content. This is another reason why you don't want to post for the sake of posting when you don't have anything to say or have any good images. If you have mediocre posts, it's going to put the influencer off. Remember, they are going to be putting up your post on their account in this scenario. So, they have to feel good about doing so, and they have to be able to do so without worrying about losing followers. Another thing to keep in mind is to avoid anything that's controversial.

Instagram uses a little icon that looks like a paper airplane that you can tap on to check your messages. It is found on the top right corner of your feed. When you tap on this, you can check messages that you have sent or received.

Gasoline On Fire

Actually, sending a message on Instagram is pretty straightforward. Begin by tapping the little icon that looks like a paper airplane. Then tap the + icon. You are going to find this in the upper right corner of your screen. After you've done this, the next step is to select the person or Instagram account if it's a business that you want to send the message to. Then select "next" and type out your message. You are allowed to include a disappearing photo or video in the message, but you're not recommended to do that for this purpose. We are not doing this for fun but for business. So, you want to be completely straightforward and direct with the person that you're contacting. Once you have typed out your message, saying exactly what you want to say, the final step is to hit the "send" button. Then, you can just sit back and wait for them to respond.

Gasoline On Fire

Before you do this, however, you want to make sure that you have the post you want them to put up already perfected and ready to go. We can't know ahead of time when they will write you back, and how much of lead time they are going to give you. So you have to be ready ahead of time. Also, they are probably going to want to see your post before they accept the deal and put it up on their feed.

It's also possible that they may want you to make modifications. Unless the modifications are totally dramatic and unacceptable, you're probably going to want to go along with what they recommend. Keep in mind that they know their own audience and you don't. So, be willing to take any advice given.

The method of sharing another person's post or page is called a "shoutout". So, you might want to use that terminology when contacting them, and ask them what they will charge for a shoutout.

Gasoline On Fire

When working with smaller accounts, say in the 15,000 - 50,000 followers range, you can propose a trade if you have already built up a certain number of followers. You don't want to be suggesting this if you are just starting out and only have 200 followers. That is not going to be worth it for them. But once you get up to 5,000 or more followers, then you can start considering it as an offer. The gist of this is a straight trade – you can suggest that, in exchange for them giving you a shoutout, you will do the same for them.

One trick you can use if you have a smaller number of followers is to offer more shoutouts for them in exchange for them giving you a shoutout. Try this in proportion to the difference in the number of followers gained. So, if you have 5,000 followers and you're trying to work a deal with someone that has 10,000 - 12,000 followers, tell them that you'll give them 2 shoutouts within one week in exchange for them giving you one shoutout. Or if they had 16,000 followers, offer them 3 shoutouts on your end.

Many large influencers won't respond to direct messages. In that case, you'll want to try email, or if they have **KIK** messaging contact info, try that. Large influencers are going to be getting inundated by direct messages from fans, so simply may avoid them altogether.

Let people Know Who the Post is From

When you are using one of these methods, you are going to be having your post appear in front of a large number of people that are not aware of your brand, account, or products. So, it's important to have more than just a caption. You want to get them to become aware of who you are (even if it's a feature account) and your logo to raise brand awareness. So, include the logo and your Instagram account name that starts with @ at the top of or the bottom of the caption.

Shoutout Trains

Another powerful tool you can utilize is a so-called "shoutout train" or shoutout group. In this case, you want to get several Instagram accounts together to share shoutouts in succession over a short time period. So, you get one person to give you a shoutout in exchange for you giving them a shoutout. Then, a second person will give the first person a shoutout, followed by a third account giving the second one a shoutout, in succession. You could even close the loop by having the last account give you a shoutout as well, and you doing the same for them. That way, multiple shoutouts go out over a short-time period generating a lot of traffic to everyone involved. This is a kind of "I'll scratch your back if you scratch mine" arrangement that is mutually beneficial to everyone involved.

Always Add Value

Remember one of the keys for shoutouts or buying posts is that you need to have your value in sync with the other accounts you are trying to leverage on. So, you need to make sure that the content on their Instagram accounts is a good match to the content that you are offering. Here is one idea – many people that follow a ketogenic diet also engage in intermittent fasting. So, if you had a Ketogenic Diet book that you were selling, you could find an Instagram account on intermittent fasting and approach them about paying for them to put up a post on your behalf or working out a "shoutout" deal. It would be perfectly complementary. If someone else had an Instagram account on auto repair, even if they had 10 million followers, trying to work a deal with them would be completely random and a waste of time. It would be better to find a directly-related account that only had 2,500 followers.

Other Ways to Pay for Influencers

There are other techniques that you can use. For example, you can pay an influencer to simply post about you with a recommendation that their followers follow you. So, in this case, you wouldn't make any post for them to use.

Another method which would be quite effective, but may cost more, is to have them make a video for an Instagram story. They could simply talk about your account for 10-15 seconds, and recommend to their followers that they follow you.

You can also have influencers take a screenshot of your page and post that with a few recent images from your account, and a recommendation for a follow.

When an Instagram influencer is making a recommendation for a follow, you want to have them use the word *favorite*. Using a specific example, if the "intermittent fasting" account were recommending you, they could say something like "Follow my FAVORITE Keto Diet page".

Be Ready for New Followers

Have two posts ready to go after your post goes up on an influencer's page. Post the first one about 30 minutes after yours has gone live on the influencer's page. Then post another one about 3 - 5 hours later. You want to make sure that new followers get engaged with your account right away.

Pricing Ranges

Generally, influencers are going to charge more money the more followers they have, regardless of engagement rate. For an account that has 100,000 or more followers but less than a half-million, you can expect to pay in the range of $20 - $35. For those with one million or more followers, you are going to be looking at something on the order of $250 and up in price.

One way that you can get shoutouts or paid postings for a lower price is to limit the total number of hours that the post is up for. This works out perfectly fine because if you can have the post up during the most active hours for the account, you are going to get the traffic anyway. Consider asking for prices for 24-hour, 12-hour, and 6-hour postings.

Have Influencers Put Up Your Website Link in Their Bio

Another option you can pursue is to have an influencer post your sales funnel link in their bio. This way, you can leverage on their huge following to get direct traffic to your website, and hopefully, there will be a lot of signups to your email list. In order to utilize this method, you are going to want to use larger-account influencers. So don't waste time contacting smaller accounts that have 50,000 followers or less. Generally speaking, you are going to want to look for influencers that have 100,000, and up to a million or more followers.

The advantage of this is not only having a large number of followers, but you are leveraging on the trust that the influencer has with their audience. Someone who has 100,000 or more followers is someone who has cultivated an audience for over a long time period. The audience is going to take their recommendations for Instagram pages, products, and services very seriously. This technique can help you generate hundreds of website unique hits over a short time period.

Gasoline On Fire

Influencers are going to charge more for this type of service, since they are going to have to put your link in their bio for a specific time period. You are going to want to have a well-converting sales funnel before you do this, so that it's not a wasted opportunity.

You can do some testing by using smaller accounts at first, in order to make sure that your sales funnel is set up properly – that is, it converts people to first signup for your email list, and second, they buy your product at reasonable rates. You don't want to spend $500 to drive traffic from a large-account Instagram page and then only make $200 back!

Chapter 10: Email-List Building and Conversions

Some things never change, and today, building your email list is going to be one of the most important things that you can do in order to sell your products. In this chapter, we are going to review the basics used for successful email-list building for those who are unfamiliar with it. You might even need a brush up if you have some familiarity with email list building. We are also going to talk about having a sale funnel that converts well.

Choosing an Email Service

There are many good email autoresponders that are available. If you are relatively new to this, you may not know what an "autoresponder" is. Basically, this is a set of emails that you have set to automatically sent out at specific time intervals after someone signs up to join your list. Typically, the first email is sent out immediately when they fill out the form and join. Then they receive the other emails in sequence at time delays you select ahead of time. This has to be done automatically. You certainly aren't going to be manually sending emails to hundreds of people. That is why there are services that will do this for you.

I do recommend **ClickFunnels** for building your sales funnels and lead pages. They do have a system built in to send emails as well, and you can use that if you don't want to spend the extra money for another service. It is a bit limited, however, and recently, they began offering a new upgrade that includes a more standardized list-building protocol with more features. But you have to pay more for that, and you can get other services at lower prices, and they are easily integrated into ClickFunnels.

One of the oldest and most popular email services used by online marketers is **Aweber**. You can sign up for Aweber for $19 a month and build multiple email lists on your account.

What you are going to want to do in the case of Aweber, is to use a legacy follow-up series.

Other good mail services include the very popular **Get Response, Mail Chimp,** and **Constant Contact.** Of all of these, my personal preference is Aweber, but you will have to pick the one you like the best. All of them can be integrated easily into ClickFunnels and some have their own lead pages. I like ClickFunnels the best, however. It's designed by actual online marketers who made their first money as affiliates for Clickbank, so they know exactly how to set everything up. Secondly, you can use ClickFunnels to build out entire websites that look fantastic by just using their visual drag and drop tools.

No matter what service you end up with, it's not worth it to spend a large amount of time worrying about which one to choose. They all work for the basic purpose of automatically sending out emails to your list. That is why I like Aweber. it's got all the basic features, and is easy to use and set up. But it really doesn't matter that much, so just pick the one you prefer.

What to Write in Your Emails

Far more important than the service provider you select is WHAT you include as content in your emails. My first tip is that you should not make your emails fancy. Although you can use HTML in emails nowadays to make them look fancy and professional, you actually don't want them to look very fancy. The purpose of using email marketing is to establish a personal connection to the customer. Are your friends sending you slick, professionally-produced emails, or do they simply type in some text, maybe drop in a YouTube video and hit send? It's probably the latter.

So, keep that in mind before you start – you want to write your emails as if you are sending them to a friend. Try a visualization exercise. Do some research on who the typical customer is for your product or service. Once you have a picture in your mind of who they are and what they are like (and it should be more than a picture – if possible use actual data), then think of a personal friend or family member that fits that demographic. Then write your emails as if you are writing directly to them.

So, what is the first piece of advice that goes beyond that? It's to avoid the hard sell. Don't open with a cheesy sales pitch. You are going to want to provide valuable content in your emails, with the sales pitch being secondary.

And, actually, by providing valuable content, you are doing your sales pitch. The idea here is that you are building trust with your readers by giving them value.

In your first email, you want to start off by describing a problem. So, you have presumably done some research on the market for your product, and you know what their top problems are. So in your first email, write as if you are writing an email to your friend, and describe a problem that they are experiencing. After you spent a paragraph writing that, then offer the solution to the problem or describe some tips and tricks to help them with that.

Then, in the very last paragraph, you can recommend that they check out the product, to have a look at the product you are pitching – all casual and not salesy. Casually say that if they would like more help with problems related to X, then they should contact you.

How Often to Send Emails

The next question we are going to face is wondering how often to send emails. Certainly, every other day is acceptable, but I often send the first three every single day in a row, then I taper it off. The reason is, when the prospect is "hot", they are most likely to buy in the immediate aftermath of signing up for the email newsletter. So, as they say, "strike when the iron is hot". You don't want to bombard them too much. So, at least after the first week, taper it off to every few days of messaging.

You want to keep most of your emails low-key and friendly, with casual references to the product you're recommending. After you've sent 3 emails, then you can send one short email with a hard sell, directly recommending that they purchase the product.

In all cases, make sure you have plenty of links to the sales page. These should stand out. One way that is often used to do this is to type something along these lines:

>>>>> Click here to learn more about X <<<<<

You can also put links in a "P.S." after you sign off. For example:

Best,

Jason

1. P.S.: To solve your acne problems, I highly recommend X.

Where "X" is the name of the product with a hyperlink. Remember our discussion of call-to-action? It applies here. You need to give your customers a chance to actually buy the product and make sure it's clear to them how they go about doing so. You don't want to lose buyers who are ready to take action, but can't clearly find out how to do it from your text.

Cross Promotion and Broadcasts

Once you have an email list put together, the list itself becomes valuable. You will want to continuously add people to your list from various sources. You can use the list to get sales from other products that are related to your main subject area. You can do this in one or two ways: One way that I prefer is that a month or two down the line after they have initially signed up to your email list, you send them an email recommending the related product.

A second method you can use is to send a "broadcast" email. That is an email that goes out to your entire list at the same time. This can be great for generating large amounts of money over a short time period. So, in your broadcast message, you pitch the second product.

Another technique that can be used is to move people off your initial list and put them on a second email list of buyers only after they have purchased the product. You can then start pitching a second product to them, and then your original list will be cleared of buyers, so you could broadcast a hard sell of the original product to try and get them to finally make a move on the purchase.

Optimizing your Sales Funnel

Having good sales funnel is going to be the key to making sure that you earn money from your efforts on Instagram. The first thing that the sales funnel must have is that it must be mobile-friendly. One of the things I like about ClickFunnels that I mentioned earlier is that it allows you to see what the page looks like on a mobile device while you are in the design phase. Again, you don't want a non-mobile optimized page that is hard to see and read on a phone.

Keep your design of the landing page simple. The first element of your landing page is going to be a clear and readable headline. There should be a sub-headline that the user sees first at the top of the page. The sub-headline should be in a large enough font to be able to be quickly and clearly read. It should tell the user WHAT they are getting when signing up for the email list. So, say something like:

"Grab this FREE Report!"

Then you have your main headline. The main headline is going to be a three-line sales pitch that explains how your guide or free report or video (or it can be a free webinar) is going to help them solve some problem in their life related to your main product. There are many different approaches that can be used for writing your headline, and you can do research online to find many examples. But if you have heard of Adam Short, he recommends three very good leading statements:

- Discover How…
- Who else wants…
- Secret revealed…

Then, you will want to provide two to three benefits to the user solving their problems, followed by a specific time frame and the word "guaranteed". For example:

Discover how you can lose weight fast, have more energy, and lower your cholesterol using the Keto diet in 14 days or less. Guaranteed!

Your landing page should also either be accompanied by a high-quality image or a video pitching the product – but don't do a hard sell. Remember, you are only trying to get them to give their email address in exchange for something free at this point.

Many marketers utilize scarcity. You can claim that the offer is only available for a limited amount of time, and only for Instagram users. A good visual demonstration of scarcity is to include a countdown counting clock at the bottom of the web page. That will get people to sign up immediately rather than having fence sitters decide they might come back later to check it out.

If you are using a photo on this page, make sure that it's a high-quality image. Remember, we are setting up a landing page that is coming directly from Instagram where users have been spending their day looking at high-quality images.

Gasoline On Fire

A second point is, you don't want to actually sell anything on the landing page. People don't like it when they are being hard sold, and the landing page is no exception. You need to presell people or warm them up first. So, all you are going to do on the landing page is to make a free offer in exchange for the email. Once you've got their email address, you can start proposing that they take a look at the product or products you are promoting.

The more expensive the product, the more effort you're going to have to put into preselling. If the product is very expensive ($500 or more), a free webinar is a good way to promote it. Many affiliate products that are expensive allow you to link to a pre-recorded webinar, and some will even do live webinars for you if you can generate a large number of visitors.

The Thank You Page

The next step in your funnel is a so-called "Thank You" page. This is a page that your users go to immediately after signing up for the newsletter. The Thank You page can include a link that they can use to download their free product. It can also include a sales pitch for the product if the product does not cost more than $250. You have three options here if you are an affiliate, and they can even be mixed together if you like. You can have a straight sales page in the form of a standard sales letter. If possible, you can link directly to the order form of the product using buttons. If that is not available, then you can link to the sales page of the vendor.

Of course, it's not a good idea to have a long sales letter that links to another long sales letter, so what you might want to do instead is briefly suggest the product, and then have a button that takes them to the sales page.

Including a video can be very helpful. If you have a solid video, you can have this at the front and center on your Thank You page. The video can be a "video sales letter" that pitches the product directly, or it could be a promotional video supplied by the vendor. Check with the vendor – many have pre-made videos they allow affiliates to use to promote their product. Then, below the video, you have a "call-to-action" button that says "Learn More About X", "Get Instant Access", or "Buy X Here". You can also make it "loud", for example, say something like "YES, JASON! SEND ME MY COPY OF X FOR IMMEDIATE DOWNLOAD!". That seems silly to many people, but it's actually very effective. Make sure that your "Buy" button is readily accessible. If people have to scroll down to see it, many might miss it entirely. They might scroll down or be scrolling up and down across the page quickly and end up missing it.

Always keep in mind the mobile experience. Later, when people are clicking on links in their emails, they might visit your page from a desktop computer. However, when they first land on the page, they are coming from Instagram and so will be using their mobile phone. So, make sure the button looks good on your phone as well as on the desktop. ClickFunnels allows you to specify that elements on your page are desktop and mobile only. So, if you have to, create separate buttons for each. You don't want an awkward looking multi-line button on your mobile version of the Thank You page.

A video review made by you can be a very effective sales tool as well. You can make the video by either demonstrating the product or simply talk about it and what it has done for you using a video that is about 5 minutes or so in length, that can even be shot using your smartphone. If the product is a digital one, it is good to shoot a video that shows it on the screen. The point is to give it a sincere review. Many vendors will provide review copies of the product – or you can purchase it using your own affiliate link to, in effect, get a discount. You will have to contact the vendor to ask. Many vendors provide review copies, but some will refuse. But it's good to actually go through the product so that your review sounds real and authentic.

Make Related Offers

You want to maximize the amount of money you can earn off one customer, and so, you don't want to be satisfied with one sale. If they purchase an item, you want to direct them to other sales pages. We mentioned using upselling and downselling before, but you can also direct them to a cross-selling pitch page as well. Often, you want to do this when they already have their credit card out. People are more warmed up to the idea of making more purchases immediately after they've bought the first product. So, what you can do is to offer a chance to buy a related product once they've completed their purchase. So, if we were selling dog training videos, after they're completely done with the purchase, you can send them to a page that offers dog biscuits or toys at a discounted price.

The Question of Double Opt-In

Due to concerns over spam, email services like Aweber implemented a system called "double opt-in". What this means is that, when someone signs up for your email newsletter, they don't get an email from you – they get one from the email service. So, using Aweber as the example, they receive an email from Aweber and it says "confirm your subscription".

Gasoline On Fire

While the email services strongly recommend double opt-in, if you see that a lot of people are signing up for your email list but it says "unconfirmed", then you need to shut double opt-in off.

The problems with double optin are that it puts an obscure additional step in front of the customer. Many times, the opt-in requests email, which comes not from you but from the mailing service, ends up in a spam or promotions folder, and so is simply ignored. Some people won't know what it's about. If they are not into internet marketing, they aren't going to have any idea what Aweber or Mail Chimp is.

In my experience, I have found that turning off double opt-in is simply a better and more effective approach. The idea that someone is going to complain after seeing your Instagram account and becoming a follower, and then voluntarily giving you their email address – that simply doesn't fly in my view. I've never had complaints of spamming turning off double opt-in, and it ensures that they actually receive your email and at least open the first one.

Summary: Steps to use

Make sure you follow these steps when marketing your products.

- Put the URL for your landing page on your Instagram bio.

- The landing page will offer a FREE product in exchange for their email address.

- The free product can be a short book in PDF format that they can download. It can be a video training guide, or it can be a seat at a free webinar. For more expensive products, a webinar or even a physical book can be used. For a physical book, you can have the book given free, but they have to pay shipping and handling fees.

- When they sign up giving you their email, then take them to a Thank You page.

- The Thank You page will have a download link for the free offer.

- It will also have a pitch for the product. It can be a video, a sales page, or a simple button to take them to a sales page.

- Send them an email follow-up sequence. It should have at least 7 emails.

- Send the first emails in the following way: Immediately, 1 day later, 2 days later.

- After that, spread them out a little bit, leaving a gap of a couple of days between emails so that they don't feel spammed.

- After they buy your product, offer them related products.

This is a proven formula, so if it's not working for you, then there needs to be some troubleshooting. Some things to look at:

- Make sure the visual setup of your landing page and thank you page is good. It should be pleasing to look at, have subtle colors that match and aren't high contrast and include high-quality images. Have other people check out the pages – both on desktop and mobile, to give their opinions.

- Check your headlines. If you don't have a good headline, that would be a problem. Make sure it conveys the information we discussed above, but also make sure it's not too long. A really long headline on mobile could be a problem.

- Make sure it's clear that people get a free offer when they sign up.

- Check every level of your funnel. Are people opening the emails? Are they clicking from each email? Do they sign up but never open the emails? It's important to pinpoint where you're having problems along the funnel.

PLR Products

Some people who are using affiliate marketing aren't sure how to go about offering a free giveaway in exchange for signing up. In this case, check out PLR or private label rights websites. They sell products in various niches, including PDF books (relatively short ones, say, 50 pages), video training, and even software products. You can use many of these as free promotional giveaways and don't have to tell anyone you didn't create it (that's why they are called "private label"). Most of them are of high quality, considering that you are giving them away for free. Your customers won't feel cheated since it's free, and most that I have seen are of decent quality. Before you go ahead and offer it, though, you will definitely want to evaluate it and make sure it's up to the standards that you're setting.

Chapter 11: Growing your Following —QuickTips

In this chapter, we are going to quickly gather up everything we've suggested and put together a plan that anyone can follow to grow their Instagram account.

Remember that the foundation for success is to post quality content. From here, we suggest the following steps:

- Post images about 2 - 3 times per day.
- If you don't have something of QUALITY to post, don't force yourself to post. Putting up low-quality material will hurt your efforts more than missing a day of posting.

- Don't rely on just posting images. Use short video clips to post to your story. Talk about the business or products you offer.

- Have a sales funnel, landing page, and email autoresponder setup BEFORE you even set up your Instagram account.

- Don't use a personal Instagram account. Make it a business or feature account. You can set up more than one feature account and use them all to drive traffic.

- You can trade shoutouts with small accounts to help build followers in the beginning.

- As you grow, start looking for paid postings and shoutouts.

- Try different methods – so look to buy traffic from Instagram accounts of different sizes, and try shoutouts and have them post your link in their bio.

- Don't spam, so limit your posts to about 3 per day.

- Always stay relevant. This is a business account, so never clutter up your account with personal postings. Keep a separate personal account for that.

- Get a professionally-designed logo if you can't do it yourself.

- Have a solid free offer on your landing page.

Conclusion

Thank you for reading this book!

If you are new to Instagram, I hope that it has opened up a new world of opportunities to help you promote your business.

If you are an experienced user on Instagram, but haven't been sure how to use it for your own business, I hope that it's helped you get specific direction on what you need to do in order to start leveraging on the power of Instagram to get customers.

One thing is for sure, while Facebook seems to be fading a bit in user engagement, and Twitter is even losing users, Instagram continues to grow and has a very high user engagement. You can promote to

millions of people at a low cost and get instant results once you've built up a following.

Whatever path you choose, I advise following your passion. You have to be interested in what you're posting about; otherwise, posting 3 times a day on Instagram is going to get tedious, and it won't come across as well.

In any case, I wish everyone success! Please drop by Amazon and leave a review of this book! Thanks again!

Connect with us on our Facebook page

www.facebook.com/bluesourceandfriends and stay

tuned to our latest book promotions and free

giveaways.